SCHOLASTIC FIRST DISCOVERY

P9-DDB-307

Night Creatures

Created by Gallimard Jeunesse
and Sylvaine Peyrols
Illustrated by Sylvaine Peyrols

SCHOLASTIC ·Ｑ· REFERENCE
an imprint of

It is nighttime.

The owl wakes up.

The owl flies silently.

The circle of feathers
around the owl's eyes
help it hear
the slightest sound.

The owl's gaze is fixed.
But it can turn its head in all directions.

Its four long talons pierce its prey,
who die without suffering.

The little hooks on the tip of each
feather muffle the noise of
the owl's beating wings.

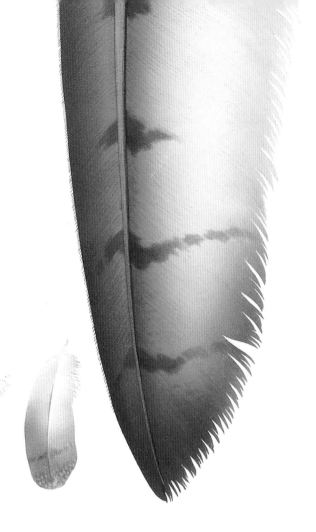

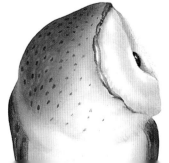

At night, the owl
hunts silently
in the fields.

At the
slightest sound,
the owl flies
lower . . .

Its four long talons pierce its prey,
who die without suffering.

The little hooks on the tip of each
feather muffle the noise of
the owl's beating wings.

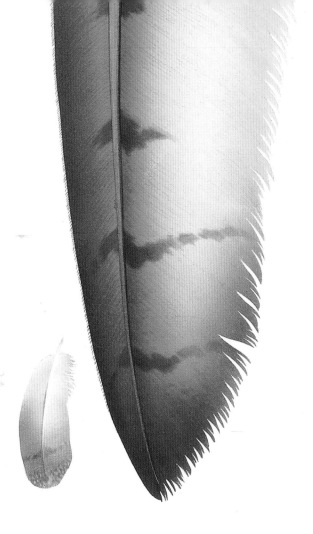

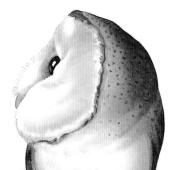

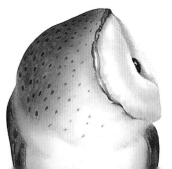

. . .and captures
a mouse! The mouse
never heard the owl coming!

Vole   **Mouse**   **Shrew**   **Field mouse**   **Sparrow**

The owl swallows small
animals without chewing.

The owl digests its food.
It coughs up what it can't digest.

An owl has coughed up this pellet
of bone, fur, and feathers.

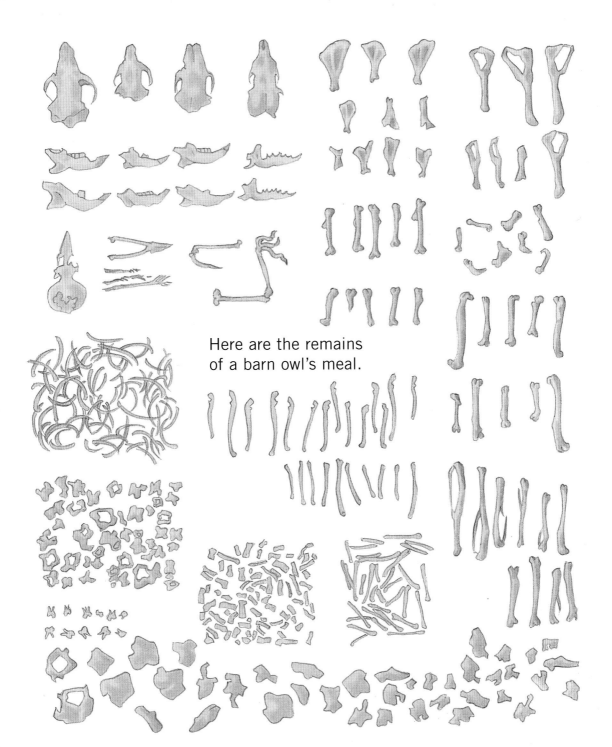

Here are the remains
of a barn owl's meal.

The female owl lays two to six eggs. She keeps them warm
and never leaves them. Her mate brings her food.

At one year old,
male and female owls
mate and remain together for life.

Female owls do not make a nest. Instead they
lay their eggs on pellets and other debris.

Owlets are blind for the first 15 days.
They are born with down.
After one month, they grow feathers.

The mother owl stays with her owlets
until they have opened their eyes
and lost their down.

The eggs are laid in stages over several days.
The owlets are born one after the other.

The parents
hunt all
night . . .

. . . to find food for
their hungry owlets.

Bats are also night creatures. At twilight, their sharp cries fill the air.

They are
ready to hunt
for food.

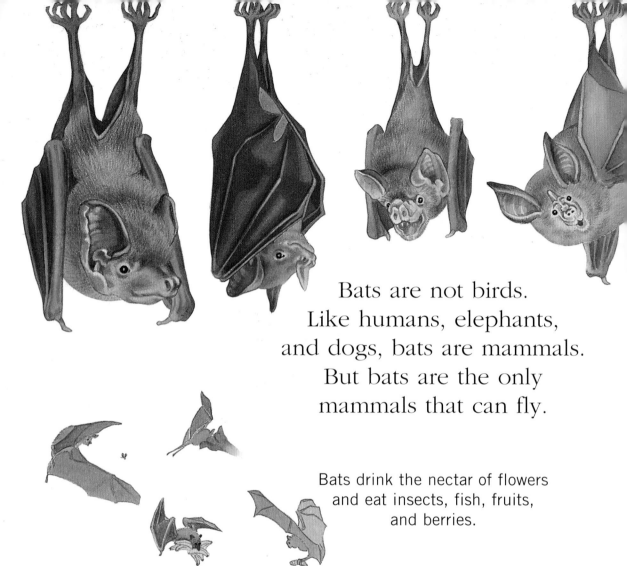

Bats are not birds.
Like humans, elephants,
and dogs, bats are mammals.
But bats are the only
mammals that can fly.

Bats drink the nectar of flowers
and eat insects, fish, fruits,
and berries.

Noctule bat

Javelin bat

Common vampire bat

Horseshoe bat

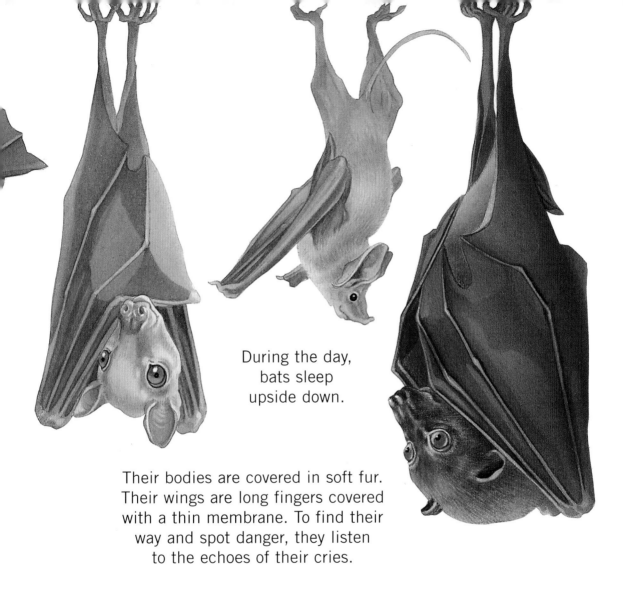

During the day,
bats sleep
upside down.

Their bodies are covered in soft fur.
Their wings are long fingers covered
with a thin membrane. To find their
way and spot danger, they listen
to the echoes of their cries.

Epauletted bat

Rat-tailed bat

**Madagascan
flying fox**

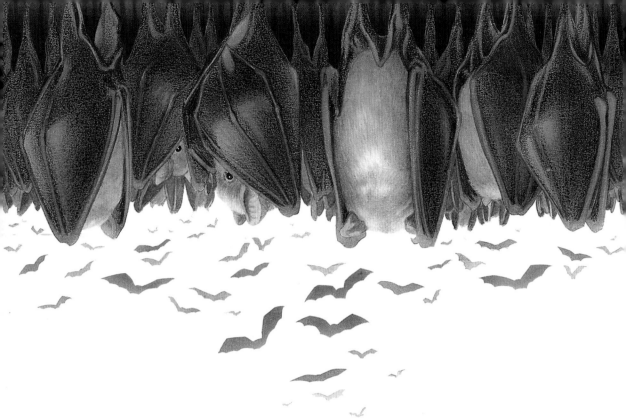

In winter, most bats
hibernate in caves.
They wrap themselves
in their wings
to stay warm.

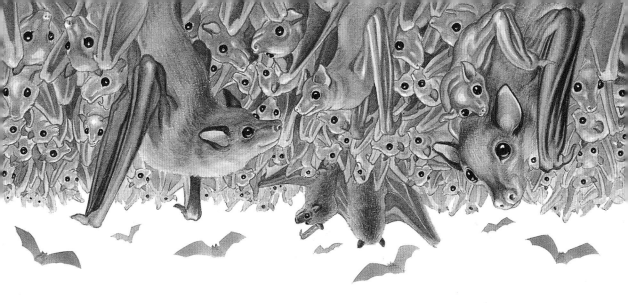

In summer, bats gather
together and form nurseries.
When the mother bat
returns from hunting, she
recognizes her young by
its cry and its smell.

The female bat only has
one pup per year
The pup attaches
itself to its
mother's fur.

Do you see the differences between these two owls?

Eagle owl

This owl has two feathery tufts on its head.

Owls with tufts

Owls without tufts

Burrowing owl

This owl has no tufts.

Here are some other nocturnal birds.
There are 300 species of nocturnal birds
in the world!

The **kiwi** is the only
nocturnal bird
that can't fly.

The **frogmouth**
lives in
the Philippines
and Australia.

The **oilbird**
lives in
South America.

The **nightjar** lives
throughout
the world except
in polar regions.

The **kakapo** parrot
lives in
New Zealand.
It flies very badly.